Cover: Pallid Caique
Pionites melanocephala pallida

Endpapers: Lesson's or Lilacine Amazon Parrot
Amazona autumnalis lilacina

HOWELL

Beginner's guide to

Parrots

Greg Jennings

Editor
Dennis Kelsey-Wood

HOWELL BOOK HOUSE Inc.
230 Park Avenue
New York, N.Y. 10169

Library of Congress Cataloging-in-Publication Data

Jennings, Greg.
  Howell beginner's guide to parrots.

  Bibliography: p.
  Summary: A guide to caring for various parrot species as pets in the home.
    1. Parrots–Juvenile literature. [1. Parrots]
I. Kelsey-Wood, Dennis.   II. Title.   III. Title:
Beginner's guide to parrots.
SF473.P3J46   1985   636.6′865   85-21892
ISBN 0-87605-940-X

Book design by Routedale Ltd, Cornwall, England
Printed in Hong Kong through Bookbuilders Ltd

*All photographs © Colorbank except for
pp 25, 38 & 40 © Paradise Press*

Contents

Introduction

Parrots form one of the most instantly recognizable groups of birds, varying in size from the tiny Pigmy Parrots *Micropsitta* species barely 9 cm (4 in) long, to the huge Hyacinthine Macaws *Anodorhynchus hyacinthinus* which are ten times larger. While many of these birds are colorful, they all possess certain anatomical features in common, such as the arrangement of their mandibles, which are significant for classificatory purposes. The upper part of their powerful beak curves down distinctively over the lower bill and the tongue itself is relatively large and fleshy, bleeding profusely if it is damaged.

The perching grip of all parrots is quite unusual, but not unique, in the avian world. Two toes are directed forwards over a perch while the other two are positioned behind. Technically known as zygodactyl, this characteristic is shared with cuckoos and similar birds belonging to the Order Cuculiformes, which are accepted as probably being the closest relatives of parrots. Most parrots can use their feet to hold items up to their beaks; an exception is the Budgerigar *Melopsittacus undulatus*. This behavior is especially seen with food, such as a piece of fruit, that is too large to be eaten at a single bite.

Lesson's Amazon Parrot is a close relative of the Yellow-cheeked Amazon which is a popular pet in the USA.

7

Explanation of Classification.

The purpose of classification is to divide the entire animal kingdom up into a series of groups (called ranks) based on the similarities of features found within animals. In higher groups, the common characteristics are more general. The Kingdom is the term used to embrace all living forms and is subsequently divided into many phyla, whose members share common features. Phyla are separated into classes, these into orders and so on, until one reaches the individual animal or species, by which point the animals resemble each other very closely.

Over the years, as knowledge of the various animals has been expanded, it has become necessary to revise classification, particularly of the lower ranks. For this reason, differences in classification may be apparent, reflecting the extent of information on that bird or group of birds at a particular point in time. The classification used in this book is based on that proposed by Peters in the *Checklist of Birds of the World* (1937). All birds belong to the class Aves, with the order Psittaciformes embracing the psittacines (parrot-like birds), as does the family Psittacidae. Peters divides the latter category into six sub-families, of which the largest is Psittacinae and the species covered in this book all belong to this main sub-family.

The lowest two ranks, genus and species, when used together serve to identify the members of a single interbreeding group or species. Within a species, there may be one or more races which differ sufficiently to warrant them being given the rank of sub-species, and these are denoted by an extra name appearing after the species; this forms the basis of the trinomial system of classification, which is recognized internationally. It is customary to write the scientific name in italics, or the generic term if this is used alone and the usage of italics is restricted to ranks beneath and including the genus. This latter term always commences with a capital letter and the species description (the trivial name) starts with a lower case letter. The name which often appears after the specific name is that of the first person responsible for the classification of the particular bird and if its genus has subsequently been changed, then the person's name is placed in parenthesis.

A figure signifies the date when the bird was initially classified. Where a trivial name is repeated, this is referred to as the nominate race, indicating that it was the first example of the species to be classified and it is therefore an example of the 'type' but not necessarily typical of the species.

A Typical Parrot Classification Table	
Class:	Aves
Order:	Psittaciformes
Family:	Psittacidae
Sub-family:	Psittacinae
Genus:	*Eclectus* (Wagler) 1832
Species:	*Eclectus roratus*
Sub-species:	*Eclectus roratus roratus* (Muller) 1976
	Eclectus roratus vosmaeri (Rothschild) 1922
	(plus a further eight recognized sub-species)

Black-headed Caiques—expensive but fascinating birds—more suited to the aviary.

Since the order Psittaciformes is comprised of approximately 332 species, it is clearly impossible in a book of this size to cover every one of them. This title is devoted essentially to the square-tailed or 'true' parrots which are popular both as house pets and aviary birds, as well as a selection of native Australian species. The latter are essentially aviary occupants, since they do not settle well in relatively confined domestic surroundings. (Other books in this series cover particular groups of psittacines in more detail, such as cockatiels, lovebirds, cockatoos and budgerigars; a current list is featured on the back cover.)

A geographical arrangement is used here for the purpose of dividing the relatively diverse group of species included in this book. Psittacines today are concentrated in tropical areas, although formerly they enjoyed a much wider distribution. Fossilized remains of a parrot classified as *Palaeopsittacus georgei*, about 60 million years old, have been discovered in Britain, close to London at Walton-on-the-Naze, Essex. This bird appears to have resembled the present-day Senegal Parrot *Poicephalus senegalus* in size.

Legislation Affecting Parrots

The international movement of parrots from one country to another is controlled by the CITES agreement, which means that appropriate documentation must be obtained in advance from the relevant authorities. Many species of parrot are regarded as pest species in their homelands, inflicting considerable damage on crops. Exportation is a practical alternative to slaughtering such birds in order to control their numbers. The trade is controlled by quotas, in most countries, which stipulate the numbers and species that can be exported, based on field studies. Guyana, from whence many parrots destined for Britain and the United States

This Festive Amazon displays excellent health—note the clear eye, nostrils, feathers and feet—the bird's health indicators.

are obtained, operate a scheme of this nature. The revenue from governmental levies can then be used in part to fund conservation projects. Many parrots are still eaten in their native lands however, even very rare species. Indeed, in the Caribbean area, where highly endangered Amazon parrots occur, they are a popular ingredient of soup, which is reputed to ensure virility in the men who consume it.

Parrots going abroad are shipped by air in approved containers and, providing due care is given *en route*, they will arrive in good condition after the journey to begin their period of quarantine. Health controls are necessary because psittacines can be afflicted with Newcastle Disease (Fowl Pest), caused by a paramyxovirus and this infection will have devastating effects on poultry, particularly if they are not vaccinated. The quarantine period lasts about 35 days, depending on the country concerned and it is forbidden to vaccinate parrots for Newcastle Disease at any stage: no treatment is available and an affected consignment of birds are normally slaughtered, as are poultry when an outbreak occurs. Since quarantine measures have been in force, in both the United States and Britain, no spread has occurred from birds in quarantine.

Smuggled parrots are a potential source of infection however, particularly those brought into the United States illegally, across the Mexican border. Parrots

10

should thus only be purchased from reputable dealers, pet stores or aviculturists, where the origins of the bird will be known.

The other disease of special significance with regard to psittacines is psittacosis, now more correctly termed chlamydiosis. It does in fact occur in a much wider range of host creatures other than parrots and cases of human infection in many instances reveal no contact with psittacine birds. However, as a precautionary measure in United States quarantine stations, all imported psittacines are treated with tetracycline antibiotics to overcome the infection, should it be present.

Legislation concerning the importation of parrots is modified at intervals, depending on the prevailing circumstances. Current details about quarantine requirements can be obtained from the U.S.D.A. in the United States, and the M.A.F.F. in Britain, while CITES legislation is enforced by the Fish and Wildlife Service, Department of the Interior, and the Department of the Environment.

The movement of all parrots into and native species out of Australia is currently forbidden. Nevertheless, aviculturists need to be aware of domestic legislation relating to the keeping of native birds, including psittacines. Birds must only be obtained from registered sources and aviculturists have to show their official permit number in advertisements. Registration is under the control of the National Parks and Wildlife Service, whose advice should be sought in the first instance. In addition, the Council of Nature Conservation Ministers (CONCOM) restricts the movement of certain rare native species, such as the Golden-shouldered Parrot *Psephotus c. chrysopterygius*. This species has actually proved quite prolific under aviary conditions and whether preventing free interchange of stock between aviculturists in different states serves to benefit the long-term survival of a species declining in the wild, remains a controversial matter.

Purchasing Stock

Parrots are naturally inquisitive birds and even tame individuals should appear alert when approached. The condition of the feathering of newly-imported birds may be rough, but this will improve at the next molt. It may not be as easy to stop birds which are feather-pluckers from damaging their plumage. Affected areas will be sparsely covered in down, or bald. The upper part of the chest region is often a common site for plucking. The reasons for this behavior are complex and overcoming the vice depends on isolating and remedying the causes, as explained later.

On close examination of a healthy parrot, the nostrils, located above the beak, should be clear and of equal size. Enlargement of one side is a sign of a previous nasal infection in most cases. The eyes must not show any discharge and the breastbone or sternum running down the centre of the lower half of the body should be well-covered, with no distinct hollows apparent on either side of the bone. This condition is referred to as being 'light' and often indicates a chronic illness.

When handling parrots, it is advisable to wear gloves as they can inflict a painful bite. The easiest way of holding a bird is to restrain its head very gently between the first two fingers of the left hand (for a right-handed person), so that its back and wings are resting in the palm. This leaves the right-hand free to examine the bird as required.

1. Accommodation

The type of accommodation provided for parrots will be influenced by various factors, but as most psittacines are relatively destructive birds, their housing must always take their powerful beaks into account. Cages are traditionally used for house pets and breeders generally have cages for moving stock, or holding birds on a temporary basis. While there are a number of different types of cage available, it is important in the first instance to select a solid model.

In recent years, plastic has been used much more widely in the manufacture of cages. Those with detachable plastic bases are relatively easy to clean thoroughly, since the lower portion can be separated for washing, but the parrot may chew the base through the cage bars. Plastic containers for food and water are likely to be destroyed by larger species such as Amazons and Grey Parrots. In the case of cages with sheet metal bases, it is important to ensure that the parrot will not catch its toe or claw inadvertently in any gaps between the sheets of folded metal. False wire floors are also dangerous for this reason and, although not generally included in modern cages, they should be removed if present.

Second-hand cages must always be regarded with caution, unless the fate of the previous occupant is known. Indeed, all cages should be washed thoroughly in the first instance, before the bird is placed within. If any disinfectant is used, the cage must be hosed off to remove any remaining trace of the chemical. Parrots spend much of their time climbing around their cage and can easily ingest poisonous substances as a result. Older cages with brass fittings must also be viewed with caution, because a chemical reaction may occur causing the appearance of verdigris, or green rust, on the metal and this will be toxic to the parrot.

The door of the cage is an important feature. It must be substantial and preferably of the type that has to be lifted vertically prior to opening, once the nut has been removed. Parrots, being intelligent birds, will soon learn to unscrew a nut using their tongue and beak, particularly if it was not fully tightened in the first instance and, should the door just simply open, then the bird will escape into the room, possibly with fatal consequences. A padlock is a wise investment as an additional precaution.

Aviaries

It may be necessary to seek permission for the construction of an aviary and this should be checked prior to construction. The traditional outdoor aviary structure consists of a flight area with an attached shelter. Although it is possible to purchase individual components that simply need to be bolted together, the resulting structure is unlikely to be substantial enough to house the majority of psittacines, which can destroy both woodwork and aviary mesh of the incorrect gauge without difficulty. The cost of purchasing a ready-made structure suitable for housing parrots is expensive and, even in kit form, it is likely to prove cheaper and more satisfactory to build the aviary at home.

Timber, preferably 5 cm (2 in) square will make a solid framework for the aviary flight. When drawing out a plan for construction, it is preferable to construct the frames taking account of the width of the aviary mesh that will be used to clad them, with 90 cm (3 ft) being a typical dimension. The size of aviary will depend to a great extent on the birds that are to be kept. There has been a trend recently, particularly in the United States, to reduce aviary sizes to a minimum. As a guide, however, the smaller psittacines covered in this book such as the parrotlets, will do well in a flight 180 cm (6 ft) in length, whereas for most other species a length twice as long will give adequate space.

Width is less crucial, with 90 cm (3 ft) sufficing in the majority of cases. It is not essential to build a rectangular structure and decorative octagonal aviaries have gained in popularity. The main drawback of these designs is that they are, by virtue of their shape, more exposed to the elements, being open on all sides with a shelter in the middle of the structure.

The timber should be jointed, to ensure a stable structure and prevent buckling at a later date. After the joints have been cut, but before the individual lengths of wood are assembled, the timber should be treated with creosote, which will act as a weatherproofing agent. Several coats should be applied in succession and, after the final coat has dried, the frames can be made up using screws and angle bars as necessary. It will take three weeks or so before the creosote can be regarded as safe from the birds' viewpoint, but, in any event, the aim will be to prevent them having access to the woodwork of the finished structure.

The aviary wire used to cover the flight panels should be 16 gauge (16G), with maximum dimensions of 2·5 cm × 1·25 cm (1 × ½ in). This will help to exclude rodents and snakes from the aviary which will otherwise disturb, if not actually physically harm, the aviary occupants. In areas where such creatures are a persistent problem, then finer mesh is to be recommended, although it will add considerably to the cost of the structure. However, bearing in mind that rodents especially can spread disease, both to birds and humans, it could be viewed as a sensible investment.

The individual frames should be wired on their inner surfaces, which will form the interior of the flight when they are assembled. Netting staples fixed at regular intervals around the timber provide the simplest and most reliable means of attaching the wire to the frame. It is important to ensure that no exposed edges of woodwork remain and, at the same time, the sharp cut ends of the mesh must be kept out of the parrots' reach. Both these requirements can be met by allowing an excess of wire top and bottom of each frame, bending it over taut on the adjoining face and fixing it on both surfaces.

Shelter

An indoor roosting area, providing protection against bad weather and a dry feeding area, must be provided in conjunction with the outdoor flight. The shelter can be constructed largely of blockwork but a wooden sectional unit, which can be simply dismantled if required, is a more versatile option. A basic framework,

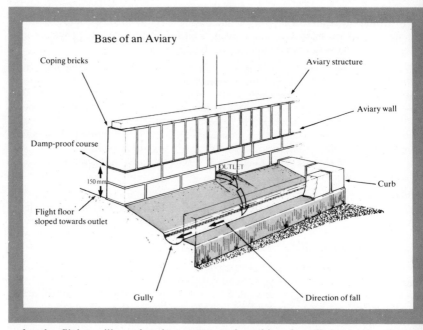

Base of an Aviary

Coping bricks

Aviary structure

Aviary wall

Damp-proof course

150 mm

OUTLET

Curb

Flight floor
sloped towards outlet

Gully

Direction of fall

as for the flight, will need to be constructed, making due allowance for the roof which should slope away from the flight. The sides of the shelter can then be clad with marine plywood which is a durable material, while at the back it will be necessary to make allowance for a door to be fitted, with a removeable window (with mesh in front), for ventilation purposes.

A second door, leading from the shelter into the outside flight will be required, irrespective of whether there is only one means of entry into the aviary. The advantage of having external doors leading into the flight and shelter is for ease of access to the aviary and results in less disturbance to the parrots. When they are breeding in the outside flight, it is preferable simply to slip into the shelter and feed them, rather than having to walk through the flight past the nest-box every time. In addition, some Amazon parrots in particular, especially tame birds with little fear of humans, may attack their owner when they are breeding. Aviary maintenance is also facilitated by the inclusion of two doors as, for example, the parrots can be shut in the shelter from the outside flight, while perches are brought through the door in the flight.

Safety porches are to be highly recommended to prevent accidental escapes as a sudden fright could cause even a tame bird to fly in panic through an open door. The safety porches need not be of such robust construction as the aviary itself, but simply a small enclosed area, the outer door of which can be shut securely prior to the aviary door being opened. If a parrot does fly out under these circumstances it will remain in the safety porch and can be readily induced to return into the aviary. It is worth fixing a secure padlock to all external doors as a clear deterrent to vandals and potential thieves. Security systems are also fitted in the case of valuable collections and some aviculturists insure their birds against such losses.

Foundations

The site chosen for the aviary needs to be located on dry ground and be relatively sheltered, yet not overhung by branches. Secure foundations are necessary, especially in areas where high winds occur and where local legislation may insist that aviaries are built to specific standards. Block construction may also be required in areas where white ants abound. The site should be cleared and then marked out carefully before excavations begin. The aviary itself should be mounted in blocks or bricks set into the ground to a minimum depth of 30 cm (1 ft). Apart from helping to ensure a strong structure, this will also serve to prevent vermin tunnelling in and gaining access to the interior of the aviary.

The base for the shelter should always be concrete, with an appropriate damp-proof course buried beneath in the form of a thick polythene sheet. The floor of the flight is also best covered with concrete, which will prove much easier to clean than grass—decreasing the likelihood of parasitic worm infections and other diseases, such as pseudotuberculosis, linked with damp ground. By allowing a suitable slope of the concrete base of the flight away from the shelter, water will drain away rapidly even after a heavy downpour and can be channelled through a small exit at the end of the flight.

Roofing

The roof of the shelter, comprised of marine plywood, should fit snugly onto the sides. Any gaps must be sealed with an appropriate water-proofing material, and the whole area tarred, before heavy-duty roofing felt is applied on top. It should overlap for 10 cm (4 in) or so down the sides of the shelter and painting it white serves to increase its lifespan, as the heat of the sun will be reflected to a much greater extent thus lessening the risk of splitting. As a final measure to ensure that the interior remains dry, guttering needs to be attached along the back of the sloping roof.

An excellent parrot aviary that uses a wall to good effect.

15

The flight itself should be covered with translucent plastic sheeting, extending at least 90 cm (3 ft) along the roof and sides closest to the shelter, to afford the parrots greater protection in adverse weather. In areas where hawks are liable to disturb the birds by diving down on to the open flight then most, if not all, of the roof will need to be enclosed. However, a small area should be left so that the parrots can bathe in the rain when the opportunity presents itself.

Perches

These can be made in the shape of a 'T' and fixed into the floor of the flight, or suspended by means of wire loops which attach firmly to the aviary framework. Perches should always run across the flight, rather than down its length. A certain variation in the diameter of the perches is to be recommended but as a guide to correct thickness, particularly for house pets living in cages, the parrot's front and back claws should not overlap, but be within about 2·5 cm (1 in) or so of each other when the bird is resting on the perch.

Perches will probably need to be replaced frequently, particularly when the parrots are in breeding condition as they are likely to be more destructive at this time. Certain woods, notably yew, lilac and laburnum may prove poisonous and so should be avoided. If in doubt about the possible toxicity of a particular tree or shrub, various books can be consulted or advice obtained from a veterinarian. Most fruit trees, such as apple and elder are safe, providing they have not been sprayed with chemicals. All branches should be washed off before being made accessible to the parrots in case they have been soiled by wild birds.

Jardine's Parrot seen at its feeding dish. This species is about 30cm in length, makes a good pet but is not the most readily available of parrots.

2. Feeding

There is now a much greater understanding of parrots' dietary needs and this is one reason underlying the improved breeding successes of recent years. The individual requirements of particular groups of psittacines are being increasingly appreciated: For example, according to American studies, Fig Parrots need a relatively high level of Vitamin K in their diet. This vitamin is normally produced in the intestines by beneficial bacteria, which are at risk from long-term antibiotic therapy. A deficiency of Vitamin K causes spontaneous hemorrhages in the body, as it is a vital part of the blood-clotting system. It is possible to supplement Vitamin K and other dietary requirements which are likely to be deficient if the parrots are kept on a diet comprised essentially of dry seed. Only Australian species, with the notable exception of the Eclectus, can be expected to reproduce successfully and repeatedly on such meagre rations.

Types of Seed

The seeds used for feeding parrots are varied and represent alternatives in their content. Cereals are low in oil (fat) and relatively high in carbohydrate, compared with the oil seeds. Maize (corn) often forms the basis of rearing foods for young parrots taken from their nests by native people. It can be a valuable source of Vitamin A, but is likely to be deficient in some of the essential amino acids which are the individual constituents of protein. Newly-imported South and Central American parrots will usually take boiled maize readily and a suitable supplement can be sprinkled over it, while they are encouraged to eat other foods.

Millets of various types and plain canary seed are also cereals commonly fed to smaller psittacines, including Australian species, but will often be sampled by other parrots as well. These seeds should be provided in a smaller container since, by virtue of their size, they will readily sink to the bottom in a standard parrot mixture—the major ingredients of which are oil seeds, notably sunflower and peanuts (groundnuts). Three distinct types of sunflower seed can be recognized, with the striped variety most readily available. Strains of sunflower are grown commercially for their oil content being used, for example, in the manufacture of margarine, whereas for parrot food the relative level of protein is more significant. White sunflower seed is preferable, since it has a relatively low oil content and a higher protein level than striped sunflower. However, it is more expensive because the yield is lower. Black strains of sunflower seed are occasionally included in mixtures but are not generally popular.

Since the mid-1970's, pine nuts have been available in Britain from specialist seed merchants as parrot food. They can also be obtained in the United States and elsewhere, but command quite a high price compared with sunflower seed.

A male Brown-necked parrot *Poicephalus robustus fuscicollis*. This rarely seen 30cm parrot has a macaw-like bill. They are from West Africa.

Gathered wild, these nuts are very popular with most species, being a more natural food than sunflower. The Thick-billed Parrot *Rhynchopsitta pachyrhyncha* for example, feeds largely in pine forests through its natural range. The smaller grades of Chinese pine nut are ideal for psittacines with less powerful bills and can be purchased separately and mixed in with other seeds. Occasionally, damaged nuts in a consignment may show signs of a greenish mold; such batches should not be purchased since it is very easy, even with care, to feed the contaminated nuts accidentally.

While the effects of this mold are not well-documented, peanuts can prove a great threat to a parrot's health if they are contaminated by *Aspergillus flavus*. They then become a source of the deadly fungal poison, aflatoxin, which has severe effects on liver function. Great care must always be taken when feeding peanuts either loose or in their shells. Those grades sold for human, rather than pet consumption are undoubtedly the safest option and can be obtained from health food stores, being added to sunflower and other seeds to make one's own parrot mixture. Only a relatively few peanuts are required in a mix and those which have been salted or otherwise treated should never be used as parrot food.

A variety of other seeds are occasionally fed to psittacines. These include oats which, without their husks, are known as groats, hemp, a small, dark-colored oil seed and safflower which can be distinguished by its irregular shape and white coloration.

18

Seed should be acquired from a reputable supplier; advertisements often appear in the various avicultural magazines. When examining a sample, it should appear clean and free from dampness, with no traces of rodent droppings evident. Fodder mite can occasionally be encountered, particularly in seed that has been stored for a long period. The mites themselves are hardly visible to the naked eye, but accumulations of grayish-white debris amongst the seed is suggestive of their presence. Metal bins are probably the best means of storing seed, since it will be kept dry and out of reach of rodents. Sealed plastic bags will cause seed inside to 'sweat', with condensation soon becoming evident followed by the growth of molds.

Soaked Seed

Germinating seed does have certain nutritional advantages over dry seed for parrots. Vitamin levels increase, as do those of protein and the seed becomes more easily digested. For this reason it is commonly fed when there are chicks in the nest and to parrots recovering from illness. Some breeders offer soaked seed on a daily basis throughout the year, to contribute variation to the diet.

Soaked seed is easily prepared, simply by immersing the required quantity in hot water for a day. It must then be washed very thoroughly under a running tap,

The Mexican Double Yellow-head can make an excellent pet-or the reverse! Check on the personality before buying. Rivals the African Grey as a talker.

before being offered to the birds. Any remaining uneaten will have to be discarded at the end of the day, because molds soon develop on such seed, necessitating a separate feeding container to that used for dry seed. A wide range of seeds can be prepared in this way and, while millet sprays are a traditional favorite, mung beans and other pulses have gained rapidly in popularity as parrot food, being offered either soaked or sprouted. They can be obtained either from specialist seed merchants, or health food stores.

Fruit and Greenstuff

The majority of parrots feed naturally on both fruit and greenstuff and such items should be freely available to them on a daily basis. The range of fruit will depend to some extent on the area concerned. Mangoes are a popular fruit in season for parrots in parts of the United States and Australia. Both fruit and the seed will be eaten, but the sticky nature of mangoes means that cleanliness assumes greater importance. In Britain, sweet apple and grapes are often fed and such items can be especially useful when taming a pet bird. Although most fruits are not of great nutritional value, being comprised essentially of water, they are a useful means of feeding a powdered food supplement which will adhere readily to the moist surface. There are a number of such products available, the majority of which only contain vitamins and minerals. Those which also include amino acids are of particular value, since some of these are likely to be deficient in seed, yet are essential for the good health of the parrot.

Greenfood acts as a valuable source of Vitamin A and a regular fresh supply can be obtained from a small corner in a garden. Spinach has much in its favor, containing significant levels of Vitamins A, B1, B2 and C, as well as iron and calcium. It is easily cultivated from seed and has the additional advantage of being available throughout much of the year, including the winter when other greenfood may be in short supply. However, some strains do contain relatively high amounts of oxalic acid which could affect the absorption of calcium so one of the varieties that have low levels of this chemical should be sown in the first instance.

Feeding greenfood also provides fiber in the diet and this is of particular value for *Tanygnathus* and *Eclectus* parrots; both genera appear to consume relatively high levels of greenstuff in the wild and will readily succumb to Vitamin A deficiency if deprived of this natural source and kept on a seed diet alone. A shortage of Vitamin A is usually the trigger for the development of candidiasis, which is discussed later.

Carrots are another valuable source of fiber and Vitamin A that can be cultivated without difficulty. Strains are now available with a Vitamin A content of about 249 mg per kilogram—double the level present in normal carrots—and these are preferable. Prior to feeding, carrots and indeed all greenstuff and fruit, should be washed thoroughly and, if necessary, peeled or scrubbed.

Whenever gathering fresh foods, such as blackberries, care must be taken to ensure that the berries have not been contaminated by chemical sprays nor, in the case of low-growing plants, that they have been fouled by other animals. Roadside verges are especially hazardous as collecting areas because, apart from the likely use of weedkillers in such localities, the lead levels of the vegetation are generally higher as a result of vehicles exhaust fumes. This chemical can accumulate in the body until toxic levels are reached.

20

Grit and Cuttlefish Bone

Both these items are important sources of essential minerals, with grit also serving to assist with the digestion of food being stored in the gizzard. Not all parrots readily partake of grit, however, but it should always be available to them; a mixture of oystershell and mineralized grits is to be recommended.

Cuttlefish bone is a major source of calcium, required particularly during the breeding season for sound egg-shells and a healthy skeletal structure in the chicks. These bones are often found washed up on beaches at certain times of the year. Providing they are not contaminated with tar, cuttlefish bones can be used safely. They must be soaked for at least a week in a bucket of water, which is changed once or twice daily. After a final thorough rinse, the bones will need to be dried either in the sun or an oven before being stored or offered to the parrots. They will gnaw the soft, powdery side of the bone which can be attached to the aviary wire by means of special clips.

Food Containers

Containers which hook on to the aviary wire are probably the most common means of feeding parrots. They can be removed easily for cleaning purposes when necessary and are thus ideal for perishable foodstuffs. Some parrots will soon learn to remove the containers themselves, scattering their contents over the floor and so it may be necessary to wire the pots in place. Soft plastic containers of this type are best avoided since they will be rapidly chewed and destroyed by the larger psittacines. Metal feeding pots are available, but prove much more expensive than their plastic counterparts. As an alternative method a stout feeding table, with stainless steel bowls weighted down in concrete or wired tightly around their exteriors, can be devised for these species.

Water is best provided in a sealed vessel, otherwise it rapidly becomes fouled with seed husks, droppings and other debris. Various drinking bottles suitable for parrots can be purchased and usually the birds will drink from these without any reluctance, especially if they have a red tip or spout. Drinkers must be positioned in an easily accessible position, as water needs to be changed daily, yet be out of direct sunlight which will stimulate algal growth in the vessel. The aviary shelter is thus the best location for both water and foodstuffs. The latter will be kept dry and should be less likely to attract rodents in this position. By lining the floor of the shelter with old newspapers, it is a simple matter of replacing the sheets when they are soiled with droppings and seed husks, usually once or twice a week.

Few parrots, apart from Australian species, will readily descend to the ground to feed and seed spilt on the floor will be wasted. In order to minimize such wastage, food pots should be placed within easy reach of a perch so the parrots are not encouraged to fly directly on to the containers—scattering seed in the process! Containers must not be placed under perches, where they are likely to be soiled.

New Developments in Feeding

Apart from the comprehensive food supplements mentioned previously, the most significant advance in psittacine nutrition over the past few years has been the marketing of pelleted diets. Available largely in the United States at present, the pellets are produced in various sizes and seem quite palatable, especially to hand-

The San Domingo or Hispaniolan Amazon is a typical 'square-tailed' parrot, but is not generally available in pet stores.

reared psittacines which are much less selective in their food preferences compared with wild-caught individuals. Two distinct diets are produced in each size—a maintenance ration and a breeder grade—which contains a higher level of protein to meet the increased requirements of breeding parrots. The latter ration should be fed from the onset of the breeding season, proving a useful conditioning food. These pellets form a complete diet and overcome the serious shortcomings that will arise from a diet of seed alone. It is important that an adequate supply of water is constantly available to parrots on a pelleted ration; the only additional foodstuffs which need to be offered daily are fruit and greenstuff.

3. Breeding

Many more parrots are now being reared successfully in collections throughout the world than at any time in the past. Indeed, if pairs are kept and housed correctly, there is no reason why they should not at least attempt to nest. Patience is an important factor since, with larger parrots in particular, they may take several years to settle in new surroundings, especially if they have been imported. As a general rule, Australian species are more tolerant of a change in their surroundings than psittacines from other parts of the world but, even so, they may not lay in their first year after being moved.

It is necessary to ensure that only one pair of parrots are kept in an aviary for breeding purposes. Severe fighting and losses can be anticipated in most cases when housing breeding birds in groups. When there is a block of aviaries together, adjoining partitions between adjacent pairs must be wired on both sides, so that the parrots cannot reach each other through the mesh. If not, serious injuries, particularly to the feet and possibly the tongue, are likely to result.

Sexing

In a number of parrot species, there are visible characteristic differences, usually in the plumage, which make it possible to identify the sexes without difficulty. The most extreme example of this type is probably the Eclectus, where cock birds are predominantly green and hens are red in color. The distinction in other cases may be much more subtle. Cock psittacines generally have more dark pigment (melanin) present in their plumage than immatures and hens. For this reason, male Grey Parrots from a given area are darker on their back and wings than females. Nevertheless, this fact can be misleading unless the birds are known to originate from the same area. Grey Parrots have a wide range extending eastwards across the central part of Africa and those from the region of Zaire seem much lighter in coloration, being referred to as 'Silvers', compared with others from western areas of their distribution.

One of the past major difficulties in breeding psittacines which were not sexually dimorphic was to obtain true pairs in the first instance. Two birds of the same sex housed together will often preen each other and behave like a true pair. This problem has now been overcome with the advent of surgical or laparotomy sexing. A small probe is inserted through an incision made in the left flank, following the administration of an anesthetic to the parrot, enabling the sex organs to be viewed in situ. In experienced veterinary hands, this technique is quite safe with negligible mortality in previously healthy birds. Additionally, the technique can be of use in assessing the state of the reproductive tract and diagnosing disorders such as aspergillosis, which otherwise may be difficult to detect from an external examination.

Amongst the laboratory methods of sexing, chromosomal karyotyping is currently the best technique available being reliable even in the case of immature parrots. The chromosomes themselves include the distinctive pair of sex chromosomes, which serve to distinguish the sex of the bird. Karyotyping entails taking a cell nucleus and extracting the chromosomes, making a 'map' which can then be viewed under the microscope. In the case of hen birds, one member of the pair of sex chromosomes are much shorted than the other. Unfortunately, karyotyping is not widely-available to aviculturists.

Prior to the advent of reliable means of sexing parrots, aviculturists were forced to look for physical differences as the means of sexing their birds. Hens, for example, may appear in some instances to have flatter heads than cocks, but such distinctions cannot be relied on to distinguish pairs. However, the pelvic bone test does have a factual basis because when hens are about to lay the gap between their pelvic bones, which can be felt with care in front of the vent as two bony prominences, is enlarged. This difference is not seen in cock birds, youngsters or hens out of breeding condition, so the application of the test is rather limited. Behavioral observations of the parrots may provide a significant clue to their sex, especially when they are in breeding condition although, again, this may be deceptive. Hen *Poicephalus* parrots, for example, flare their tails open rather like a fan, especially when close to their nest-box. Cock psittacines often possess a deeper call-note than their mates.

Nest-boxes

Many parrots will roost in their nest-box throughout the year and this is to be recommended, especially in temperate climates, as protection against the elements. Although parrots, once acclimatized, can winter outside even in relatively severe weather, they are at risk from frostbite if they are allowed to roost outside on perches in the open flight.

The size of the nest-box is clearly influenced by the size of the parrot but, generally, a relatively small box is preferred. It is important that the nest-box is constructed of thick wood to withstand the onslaught of a parrot's beak. The diameter of the entrance hole should be just sufficient to admit the birds without difficulty: it can be square or round. The parrots are certain to gnaw around the hole, becoming especially destructive when in breeding condition. If the entrance hole becomes too large, the nest-box may be ignored as excessive light penetrates to the interior.

For many years, damp peat has been the favored lining material for nest-boxes yet, in spite of this, breeding parrots will often scratch much of the contents out via the entrance hole onto the aviary floor. Studies in the wild suggest that parrots may spend a considerable period of time preparing a breeding site. Under aviary conditions, gnawing is probably part of the natural breeding stimulus and for this reason pieces of untreated softwood, such as cheap battening, can be broken into short lengths and placed at the bottom of the nest-box. Here they will be whittled away by the parrots to form a natural lining on which the eggs will be laid. Any surplus will be ejected from the nest.

The location of the nest-box is rather dependent on the species concerned. Australian parrots will lay in nest-boxes positioned in relatively open surroundings, such as the outside flight, but under cover where they will be protected from he excesses of the weather. Certainly in the case of *Poicephalus* and *Pionites* species, a darkened location is necessary to stimulate breeding activity. This can be achieved by screening the outside of the aviary with dark plastic, or restricting the amount of light entering the shelter.

The Breeding Period

Once the nest-box is to her liking, the hen will take more cuttlefish bone, which must be freely available and her droppings often become larger prior to laying. Central and South American species mate with cock birds keeping one foot on the perch, whereas male parrots from other continents support themselves totally on the hen's back. Egg-laying takes place at intervals with one or two days between

Female Eclectus parrot at natural tree nesting site built into an aviary.

the appearance of each egg. Clutch size can be quite variable, ranging from two eggs in the case of *Eclectus* and *Tanygnathus* parrots to as many as six in the case of Regent Parrots and other Australian species. Four eggs probably form the usual clutch of most parrots. The hen incubates alone, but the cock may join her in the nest for periods and feeds her during this time.

The incubation period depends on the species concerned and when the hen started sitting in earnest. Many do not commence incubating until the second egg has been laid, which in turn ensures that the chicks are of a more even age when they hatch, thus improving their chances of survival.

Assuming all goes well, the chicks should fledge from about six weeks onwards, depending on the species concerned, being fed largely by the cock bird for a short time until they are eating independently. The young parrots must then be moved to separate accommodation because Australian species and *Forpus* parrotlets in particular can subsequently prove very aggressive to their chicks and may even kill them if they remain in the same quarters as the adult birds. Such behavior generally occurs in the case of more prolific psittacines, which will lay again almost immediately after producing one round of chicks.

Breeding Difficulties

Failure of eggs to hatch is a relatively common problem which can occur for two reasons, either they were not fertilized, or the embryo died in the shell. In the latter instance, the eggs appear opaque when viewed in a good light, rather than being relatively clear. The degree of humidity may have been at fault, with the eggs failing to lose sufficient water in the latter stages of incubation, causing the chicks in effect to drown; alternatively mineral deficiencies could be responsible. Indeed, any shortcomings in the diet will be emphasised when the birds are breeding, so that low hatchability, sickly chicks and feather-plucking may result from poor nutrition.

As suggested previously, a diet comprised of seed alone is deficient in various respects, especially with regard to protein and it is preferable to offer supplementary foods throughout the year and simply increase the quantities offered when there are chicks in the nest. Brown bread soaked in milk is a valuable item, since it will provide essential amino acids that are deficient in seeds. These can be passed on via the protein contained in the egg and then directly to the developing birds, thus leading to improved breeding results overall. All perishable foodstuffs must be removed daily, before they can sour.

New Developments

In recent years the use of incubators and hand-rearing has meant that more parrot chicks are being bred from a given pair, since removing the eggs will usually stimulate the parrots to nest again in a short space of time. Indeed, a few species (notably the Eclectus) will breed consistently through much of the year if conditions are favorable. It is to be recommended, however, to restrict the birds to two or three clutches. Excessive breeding is likely to lead to problems such as egg-binding. Reference to a more detailed book is advisable for those interested in hand-rearing. A wide range of diets have proved successful for this purpose and new information can be obtained from many of the avicultural periodicals produced around the world.

4. Parrots in the Home

arrots have been popular as pets for centuries and the keeping of parrots in
urope was fashionable with the nobility from the Middle Ages onwards. Henry
III (1508-1547) was just one monarch who appreciated these birds. The Grey
arrot that was kept at his palace at Hampton Court in England learnt to call the
oatman from the other side of the river, then advising that the servant should be
iven a groat for his trouble! The distinctive talking ability and mimicry of many
pecies of parrot, coupled with their gentle and confiding ways, has since attracted
any people to them as pets. Cheaper and easier to maintain in confined
rroundings compared with dogs and cats, parrots are nevertheless demanding
irds, by virtue of their natural intelligence.

nder no circumstances should a parrot of any kind be purchased if it is to be left
n its own for long periods every day. They are gregarious creatures by nature
nd will rapidly pine under such conditions. Vices like feather-plucking then
ecome evident and this habit is extremely difficult to break once it starts.

electing a Pet Parrot

n order to obtain the greatest enjoyment from having a parrot as a pet, there are
ertain basic guidelines which must be appreciated. In the first instance, the
ustralian species covered in this book cannot be considered suitable as com-
anion birds, in view of their nervous and active dispositions; they are also poor
imics. Amazon Parrots and the Grey Parrots are regarded as the best species for
ose seeking a pet. Greys are very talented talkers but can prove shy, particu-
rly in front of strangers, while Amazons have a raucous call, which is likely to
ecome apparent during the morning and late afternoon, when they naturally give
oice. Both *Pionus* and *Poicephalus* parrots can prove successful mimics and are
enerally cheaper than the preceding species in addition to being less noisy. Their
mall size and reliable temperaments makes them more suitable for an environ-
ent where children are present.

he most important point is to select a genuinely young bird, of whatever species
 chosen, preferably when it has just left the nest. The means of recognizing
nmatures of the various species are given in the next chapter; a fairly universal
eature is that young parrots have darker eyes than adult birds. With the large
umber of parrot-like birds that are now being bred annually in aviaries, it should
ot be too difficult (depending to some extent on the locality) to obtain a hand-
eared chick, which will naturally have little or no fear of humans from the outset.
lthough relatively expensive such birds are, without doubt, the best acquisition
r someone seeking a parrot which will develop into a cherished, tame and
lking pet. Given the fact that parrots should live for well over twenty years, it is

The very popular African Grey Parrots must be purchased when very young if wanted as pets.

Whilst the wire-netting seen in this photo may be adequate breeders are recommended to use heavier guage welded mesh.

much more satisfactory to wait for a suitable individual, whose age will be known rather than just buying the first one that is seen, no matter how strong the temptation.

Settling in and Taming

Having acquired a young parrot, it should be left quietly to settle in its new environment for a day or so. Its cage should be positioned on a firm base, out of direct sunlight. Seed will be spilled outside the bars of the cage so that surrounding furniture may need to be covered to prevent soiling. A check should be kept on its droppings, ensuring that it is eating properly. Difficulties in this respect are most likely to be encountered with hand-reared parrots which are not fully weaned. If possible, the diet offered should be identical to that provided during the early stages at its previous home.

There is no single correct technique for taming a parrot but, in the first instance, it can be encouraged to take titbits in the form of fruit through the cage bars. While the young bird may not accept them immediately, it should soon start to take such offerings. As the next step, it can be fed with the hand actually inside the cage. Although parrots are capable of biting hard, they do not usually attempt to use their beaks unless actually restrained physically. If they feel threatened, they will simply withdraw to the corner of the cage.

low, deliberate movements at this stage will do much to overcome the parrot's natural hesitation. Under no circumstances should the hand be pulled away rapidly, nor must the bird ever be teased with the titbit. Parrots like to have the sides of their head scratched—this is how they preen each other naturally. It is probably best to do this through the cage bars at first and then gently within the cage itself. However, if the parrot appears distressed it may be best to wait until it comes out of its cage.

The vast majority of cages are completely inadequate for housing parrots on a permanent basis, since they are too small. It is quite straightforward to make a larger structure, in the form of an inside flight or obtain cages that come in kit form. Additional panels for the latter can be purchased without difficulty, to make a more satisfactory cage. In any event, the parrot should be let out of its confines on a daily basis for periods of supervised exercise. It is sensible to obtain a pair of thick gloves for both training and restraining the bird at this stage, since even the claws can be painful on the skin if they are dug in.

The first step is to place the gloved hand stretched carefully alongside the perch and encourage the parrot to transfer across on to it, by moving slowly up and over the perch. Once the parrot readily perches on the hand, it can then be gradually withdrawn outside the cage. The bird may choose to transfer to the bars, climbing up to sit on top of the cage, which is a favorite position. There are a number of possible dangers in the average room, ranging from potentially poisonous plants to electrical wire connected to a live socket and, for such reasons, parrots must not be left alone out of their cages. They may also start to gnaw furniture, or knock over valuable ornaments.

A check must be carried out beforehand to ensure that all windows are closed and covered with mesh, signifying a physical obstruction to the bird which may otherwise not be appreciated, so the parrot flies into the glass, possibly with a fatal outcome. The door will clearly need to be kept shut and other pets, especially cats, must be removed from the room. On no account should even very tame parrots be given liberty in a garden; if they are suddenly disturbed for any reason, they are liable to panic and fly off.

Talking

Teaching a parrot to talk successfully is largely a matter of repetition. A number of companies in the United States produce cassette tapes and records to facilitate training in this respect, but unless the owner is actually in the room with the bird, to attract its attention, they will not be entirely successful. Word association is a useful tool in the trainer's repertoire. When the curtains are drawn in the room where the parrot is kept then, the phrase 'Good night' for example, can be spoken. In the morning, as the curtains are opened, the greeting 'Good morning' can be repeated. After a period of time, depending partly on the individual, the parrot should start to reciprocate these statements. Gradually a vocabulary can be built up in this way, not forgetting to repeat words learnt previously.

For owners who are worried, or have difficulty in taming and teaching their parrots to talk, a number of specialist trainers operate throughout the United States. They can be contacted via the various avicultural magazines, and will, for a fee, advise on individual cases.

5. The Species

Amazon Parrots

The genus *Amazona* is comprised of 25 species which range through much of Central and South America, as far south as Bolivia and Argentina. Amazon Parrots also occur on various islands in the Caribbean, but here most species are in serious decline; in the case of some, such as the Puerto Rican Amazon *A. vittata*, it may be too late already to prevent their extinction. These remnant populations are at risk from introduced species, human destruction of habitat and the periodic hurricanes that blow through the islands.

The recent extensive survey by Ridgely suggested, however, that the numbers of mainland Amazons, even those species which were often exported, appeared not to be in decline. Perhaps not surprisingly, the Mexican species are more commonly seen in United States collections than in Europe. Amazons have long been popular as pet birds, formerly being described as 'Green Parrots' which is the predominant color in the plumage of most species and served to distinguish them from the African Grey Parrot. They are talented mimics, but can become possessive, attaching themselves to a single member of the family, while being hostile to the remainder. If everyone shares the routine of caring for the bird from the outset, such behavior is less likely to be encountered. In the home, Amazons may

The Festive Amazon-one of the less popular of the South American Parrots.

The Blue-fronted Amazon. This species is regarded as one of the finest 'mimics' to be had as a pet but, like most similar birds, they are expensive so do purchase potential pets whilst they are young and easily tamed.

produce copious quantities of feather dust, especially when molting, and need to be sprayed daily. Human allergy can result from prolonged exposure to this dust if it builds up in the environment and daily cleaning of the cage is to be recommended.

Whenever purchasing newly-imported Amazons, particular emphasis must be placed on inspecting the eye-lids, which should open readily and the nostrils, which ought not to be blocked. It would appear that a Vitamin A deficiency can be involved in these cases; treatment with an antibiotic and dietary supplementation may overcome the problem if it is of this nature. Amazon Parrots are hardy once acclimatized and make attractive aviary inhabitants although their loud calls, often uttered early in the morning, may make them unsuitable for outside flights in built-up areas. Only the White-fronted *A. albifrons* is sexually dimorphic and surgical sexing will be necessary in order to obtain pairs of the other species. When breeding, Amazons can become quite aggressive; tail-flaring and constriction of the pupils, causing the eyes to briefly appear more colorful, are two common indicators of the onset of reproductive activity. They generally mature around three years of age and hens will rarely lay more than once in a season, unless their eggs or chicks are removed at an early stage.

The Mealy Amazons make excellent pets and are outstanding mimics-though sometimes rather noisy.

Caiques

The two species of caique are characterized by their white breasts. The Black headed Caique is more readily available to aviculturists than the White-bellied form. They are very lively birds, about 22·5 cm (9 in) in length, surprisingly destructive and quite vocal. Neither species is sexually dimorphic. In spite of their sociable natures, established pairs of caiques will occassionally attack individual and must always be kept isolated. As companion birds, they demand a great deal of attention; even aviary individuals will become quite tame. Fruit must figure prominently in their diet. Breeding successes in recent years have often been obtained when the birds have been housed in relatively dark surroundings. They can live in excess of four decades.

Black-headed Caique.

A male Spectacled or White-fronted Amazon Parrot. This species is quite popular in the USA but is not as talented as other South American parrots

Parrotlets

Only the *Forpus* Parrotlets are known to aviculture. They are small birds, predominantly green in color; seven species and a relatively large number of subspecies are recognized by taxonomists. As avicultural subjects, parrotlets are ideal for an aviary in surroundings where large and more noisy parrots could not be kept. It is safest, especially with breeding pairs, to house them in flights rather than cages because these square-tailed parrots have a deserved reputation for mutilating and actually killing their youngsters around fledging time. In an aviary the young parrotlets will be less at risk. Although not generally kept as companion birds, it is likely that a hand-reared parrotlet would settle well in the home.

Parrotlets are not regularly imported, unlike certain Amazons, but usually can be obtained without too much difficulty. Over the past few years, the attractive Yellow-faced species *F. xanthops* has become available and proved as keen as other species to reproduce, although newly-imported stock has not always proved easy to establish because of the presence of blood parasites. The acquisition of captive-bred stock is thus especially recommended in this case. Parrotlets can live for two decades or more in spite of their small size.

A pair of Yellow-faced or Spengel's Parrotlets (male on left).

Immature Dusky Parrot *Pionus fuscus*

Pionus Parrots

Various species of *Pionus* have been irregularly imported over the course of the past decade, both to the United States and Europe, with the Blue-headed *P. menstruus* being most common. They are all relatively small parrots, ranging between 22·5 cm and 27·5 cm (9-11 in) in size and lack the bright plumage of certain other psittacines. However, *Pionus* arc not dull since their plumage has an attractive sheen, most noticeable when these birds are being kept in outdoor aviaries.

Young *Pionus* parrots make ideal pets, but adults are generally nervous and will not adapt well to life in domestic surroundings. Any which show signs of wheezing may be afflicted with aspergillosis—a relatively common disease in members of this genus. None of the eight recognized species is sexually dimorphic, but numbers of *Pionus* are being reared each year in aviaries.. Some pairs prove poor parents though and the chicks will have to be removed for hand-rearing if they are neglected. It is important to ensure that the nest is easily accessible, so that it can be inspected without scaring the adult birds.

African Parrots

The Grey Parrot is best-known for its powers of mimicry yet it has also become much more widely-appreciated as an aviary bird during recent times. Pairs prove prolific, particularly when housed indoors, and here they may lay for much of the year if given a varied diet. Chicks are relatively easy to rear by hand and make delightful pets. However, adult Greys are unsuitable as pets and, because of their habit of hissing at anyone close-by, are described as 'growlers'. Grey Parrots are sensitive birds, readily given to feather-plucking. While Greys will live throughout the year in outdoor aviaries once acclimatized, newly-imported individuals should only be placed outside during the warmer months of the year. It may be necessary to bring them indoors for the first winter, if they appear uncomfortable in the colder weather.

The nine species of *Poicephalus* parrot are smaller than the Grey, ranging in size from 22·5 cm to 30 cm (9-12 in) in the case of the rare Cape Parrot *P. robustus*. Both the Senegal *P. senegalus* and Meyer's *P. meyeri* are generally available, while Jardine's Parrot *P. gulielmi* is also occasionally seen. Adult birds are usually nervous and will often retreat to the nest-box if they feel threatened, but youngsters can make delightful pets, especially if they have been hand-reared. *Poicephalus* parrots are destructive for their size, but are also relatively quiet birds whose calls consists of a series of rasping whistles. Their nest-box should be placed in a relatively dark and secluded position in the aviary; it is not uncommon for these parrots to nest during the colder months of the year in temperate climates. None of the species in the following table are sexually dimorphic; all are particularly fond of peanuts.

The African Grey (Timneh variety) is a perennial favorite.

Senegal Parrots—in spite of their somewhat menacing 'looks'—make playful pets if aquired when young. However, like all parrots, no two are quite the same in their natures.

A pair of Australian King Parrots—such birds are seldom available outside of their native country—a fact reflected by their price.

Australasian Parrots

Certain psittacines inhabit both Australia and offshore islands. The Eclectus Parrot *Eclectus roratus* is a typical example, with a small population occurring on the Cape York Peninsula, especially in the vicinity of the Iron Range. Nine other sub-species are distributed on the islands to the north and, while males are basically similar in appearance but differ in size, hens show quite marked plumage disparities.

These parrots must be provided with a varied diet including greenfood on a daily basis if they are to remain in good health. They can become noisy when breeding and cocks may be persecuted by their mates, even to the extent of being denied access to the feeding pots. Alternative feeding sites around the aviary are thus to be recommended. *Eclectus* have proved ready nesters under aviary conditions, laying clutches of two eggs. Some pairs produce offspring of the same sex over a number of rounds; hens are generally scarcer—a fact reflected by their price in Australia.

Two other genera occurring both in Australia and elsewhere are *Alisterus*, the King Parrots and *Aprosmictus*, the Red or Crimson-winged Parrots. The Australian King Parrot *A. scapularis* is less well-known outside its native country than the two related island species, particularly the Amboina *A. amboinensis* which nevertheless is still relatively scarce. All have similar habits, however, being active birds which need a long flight to show to best effect. King Parrots can be reluctant to nest, unless provided with a deep nest-box. This can be stood on the floor of the aviary, preferably on a solid base of bricks so that it will not topple over, nor get wet. A darkened location is again to be recommended.

Male Eclectus Parrot—the more brightly colored female can be seen on page 25.

Crimson-winged Parrots *A. erythropterus* are similar in their habits to King Parrots and again, when breeding, cocks can prove aggressive towards their mates. Pairs may well be double-brooded once they commence nesting, while maturity may not be attained until the third year after hatching. The island species *A. jonquillaceus*, is also seen occasionally in Europe and the United States.

The *Tanygnathus* parrots are similar to the Eclectus but are less well-known in aviculture. The Great-billed Parrot *T. megalorhynchos* is imported to the United States quite regularly along with the duller Muller's Parrot *T. sumatranus*, but never in large numbers. A few of each species are occasionally available in Britain as well as Europe. Neither species has yet been bred, but the related Blue-naped

The Red or Crimson-winged Parrot.

A pair of Blue-naped
Parrots.

One of the first Blue-
naped chicks to be bred
in Europe.

Male Spectacled Parrotlet. Many beginners mistake parrotlets for African lovebirds, to whom they bear a superficial resemblence. However, they are quite different birds.

Parrot *T. lucionensis* has nested repeatedly both in the United States and Britain. Although pairs may take several years to settle, they will then lay regularly. In Britain, pairs have double-clutched repeatedly since the initial successes were recorded in 1983. *Tanygnathus* parrots have similar needs to the Eclectus and also readily succumb to candidiasis unless their diet contains adequate levels of Vitamin A.

While Australian parrots are covered in detail in another title in this series, mention must be made here of the Pileated Parrot *Purpureicephalus spurius*. Outside Australia, this species is also referred to as the Red-Capped Parrot and shares both its common names with the rare South American parrot *Pionopsitta pileata* which occurs in Brazil and Paraguay. This latter species, seriously threatened by deforestation through its native area, is represented in a few collections. They are very different birds, however, both in appearance and habits. *Purpureicephalus* are relatively common aviary occupants although ranking amongst the more expensive Australian species. They have lively natures and delight in bathing, while their beaks will be used to attack any exposed woodwork in their flight. As breeding birds, they can be quite prolific and young birds will nest in their second year, before they have molted into adult plumage.

BREEDING SUMMARY

Parrots	Clutch size	Incubation Period	Fledging time
Amazons	2-5 eggs	27 days	8-9 weeks
Parrotlets	3-6 eggs	18 days	5-6 weeks
Pionites	3 eggs	27 days	10-11 weeks
Pionus	3 eggs	27 days	10-11 weeks
Grey Parrot	3 eggs	28 days	11-13 weeks
Poicephalus	3-4 eggs	26 days	9-10 weeks
Eclectus	2 eggs	28 days	11-12 weeks
Tanygnathus	2 eggs	28 days	10-11 weeks
King Parrots	3-4 eggs	21 days	6-7 weeks
Red-winged Parrots	3-4 eggs	21 days	6-7 weeks
Pileated Parrot	3-7 eggs	20 days	6-7 weeks

NOTE: The above figures are intended as a guide and they may well vary in individual circumstances.

AMAZON PARROTS

Species	Distinguishing Features	Immatures	Distribution	Comments
A. aestiva Blue-fronted Amazon	Blue area in head above cere variable in extent	Dark irides	From Brazil to Argentina and Paraguay	Has become less common in Europe recently.
A. albifrons White-fronted Amazon	White area on head above cere. Cock birds invariably have red primary coverts; green in hens	Yellowish tint to white area of plumage	Mexico and Costa Rica	Smallest species—26 cm (10 in) in length
A. amazonica Orange-winged Amazon	Similar to *A. aestiva* but has horn-colored bill and orange, not red, wing speculum	Dark irides	Extensive range over northern South America apart from the western seaboard	Like all amazon parrots this species will make an excellent pet if aquired at young age
A. farinosa Mealy Amazon	Relatively dull coloration very variable area of yellow in the vicinity of the crown	Dark irides	Mexico southwards to parts of Brazil and Bolivia	The largest of the mainland species at 38 cm (15 in); equally powerful voice
A. finschi Lilac-crowned Amazon	Similar to *A. viridigenalis* but red area on the head does not extend beyond crown; orange irides	Dark irides	Western Mexico	Also known as Finsch's Amazon it is generally a very docile bird—a good pet

Species	Coloration	Other features	Distribution	Notes
A. ochrocephala Yellow-fronted Amazon	Yellow on the head	Dark irides	Fractioned distribution from Mexico southwards to Peru and the Guianas.	9 sub-species including the Double yellow-head which has an almost totally yellow head when mature
A. viridigenalis Green-cheeked Amazon	Lilac on sides of head with red extending back past the eyes towards the back of the neck	Decreased area of red; dark irides	North-east Mexico	Also known as the Mexican Red-headed Parrot

CAIQUES

Species	Coloration	Other features	Distribution	Notes
P. melanocephala Black-headed Caique	Black on the top part of the head	Bill is horn, rather than black	In a broad band from Peru to the Guianas	Caiques are highly individualistic but are the more rewarding for the extra effort they may sometimes require
P. leucogaster White-bellied Caique	Orange replacing black present in *P. melanocephala*	Dark irides. Odd black feathers on the head	South of the Amazon from Peru to Brazil	

PARROTLETS

Species	Coloration	Other features	Distribution	Notes
F. xanthops Yellow-faced Parrotlet	Bright yellow head. Hens have pale blue rumps	Paler than adults	A very limited area in north-western Peru	Due to their lack of bright colors the parrotlets are not as popular as the African lovebirds but are highly regarded by many breeders
F. coelestis Pacific Parrotlet	Cocks have blue lines behind the eyes; hens are totally green in color	Paler than adults	Ecuador and Peru	
F. conspicillatus Spectacled Par.	More blue on head and around eyes of cocks	Paler than adults	Western Columbia	

PARROT SPECIES COMMONLY AVAILABLE IN THE USA AND EUROPE

AFRICAN PARROTS

Species	Distinguishing Features	Immatures	Distribution	Comments
Psittacus erithacus Grey Parrot	Gray plumage and red tail	Have gray irides	In a band across central Africa to Tanzania	The distinctive sub-species *P.e.timneh* is darker overall with a maroon, rather than a red, tail
Poicephalus gulielmi Jardine's Parrot	Green overall, with areas of orange-red plumage on the head, thighs and at the sides of the wing	Duller, lacking the orange-red markings.	Essentially as above	Also known as the Red-headed or Red-crowned Parrot
Poicephalus meyeri Meyer's Parrot	Brown back with turquoise-green rump. Variable yellow coloration on head and wings	Dark irides	Central and Southern Africa avoiding coastal areas	Six sub-species are differentiated showing marked plumage variation. Meyer's (or Brown's) parrots make colorful and affecionate pets
Poicephalus senegalus Senegal Parrot	Grayish-black head, green breast and back, with pre-dominantly yellowish-orange underparts	Dark irides	Central-West Africa	The sub-species P. s. versteri has a reddish belly. Like all members of this genus they make good pets

AUSTRALASIAN PARROTS

Eclectus roratus Eclectus	Cocks predominantly green with horn colored upper bill; hens red with purple band across lower breast and abdomen	Can be sexed in the nest. Have dark irides	Cape York Peninsula, New Guinea and surrounding islands	Ten sub-species recognized
Tanygnathus megalorhynchos Great-billed Parrot	Scalloping on the wings, blue on the rump. Predominantly green	Dark irides	Fractioned island range around the Celebes	Cocks may have black at the shoulder and large beaks
Tanygnathus lucionensis Blue-naped Parrot	Similar to previous species but smaller, with a green rump and blue at the nape of the neck	Lack the blue on the nape, dark irides	Philippines	Sexing as above
Tanygnathus sumatranus Muller's Parrot	Green with a blue rump	Resemble female with dark irides	Philippines and Celebes	Cocks have red beaks, whereas those of hens are whitish
Alisterus scapularis Australian King Parrot	Red head and underparts. Predominantly green back and wings. Hens have green heads	Have brown, not black, bills and brown irides	Eastern seaboard of Australia	Aptly named, these magnificent birds are strictly for the aviary —and the specialist
Alisterus amboinensis Amboina King Parrot	Similar to the preceding species but with reddish upper bill and prominent purple area on the back. Not sexually dimorphic	Dark irides	Western New Guinea and adjacent islands	A further member of this genus—the Green-winged—is occasionally available

47

PARROT SPECIES COMMONLY AVAILABLE IN THE USA AND EUROPE

AUSTRALASIAN PARROTS

Species	Distinguishing Features	Immatures	Distribution	Comments
Aprosmictus erythropterus Red-winged Parrot	Predominantly green head and body; black back, blue rump; prominent area of red on the wings. Hens lack the black mantle; area of red reduced	Resemble hens with dark irides	North and north-east Australia	Deep log nest is preferred. Only the hen sits but both parents feed the chicks
Aprosmictus jonquillaceus Timor Red-winged Parrot	Lacks the black coloration of the preceding species, with greenish-yellow area on wings and reduced area of red. Hens lack blue edging to plumage in the vicinity of the upper back	Pale brown irides	Occurs on Timor, Wetar and Roti in the Lesser Sunda Islands	Can be treated in all respects as in the preceding species
Purpureicephalus spurius Pileated or Red-capped Parrot	Male has red cap extending to nape. Yellow cheeks, rump and upper tail coverts. Chest and abdomen violet-blue with lower abdomen red. Rest of bird is mainly green with edges of primary feathers blue. Females are duller—especially on the head and chest	Resemble hens but with green caps	South-western Australia	The species is the only one in its genus. Its beak is narrow and less curved than in most parrots. A very colorful bird but expensive

6. Health Problems

Parrots are generally healthy birds and not difficult to maintain in good condition, particularly once they are settled in their quarters. New birds should be quarantined for at least two weeks before being placed in contact with established stock. as a precaution against the introduction of disease. Most parrots will live in excess of ten years, although clearly the age of imported stock is unlikely to be known accurately. Signs of illness are dependent to some extent on the disease but, generally, sick parrots appear dull and lethargic, usually fluffing their feathers and taking little interest in food. When showing these signs, an individual should be transferred to a warm environment, about 30°C (85°F), and veterinary advice sought without delay.

A heated hospital cage, or an infra-red lamp suspended over a cage can be used to maintain this temperature and then, following recovery, the bird should be gradually reacclimatized. In cases of bacterial infection antibiotic therapy, if commenced early, should prove successful in effecting a cure, providing the appropriate drug is used as directed. In countries such as the United States where antibiotic remedies are on open sale, it is vital to select the correct treatment since not all antibiotics are equally effective against specific bacteria.

Cuts and Bleeding

Bleeding is likely to occur if a claw is clipped too short and, for this reason, the blood supply—visible as a thin red streak extending along the claw—must always be located before nipping off the end of an overgrown nail with a stout pair of bone clippers. Similarly, if a wing has to be clipped, the flight feathers do receive a blood supply for a period, which gives their quills a pinkish tint. Cutting at this level will cause profuse bleeding. The beak can also be damaged in a similar way if it is cut carelessly. Under normal circumstances, parrots keep both their beaks and claws in shape, particularly when they have wood to gnaw. In cases where minor bleeding does occur, however, the application of a styptic pencil or a cold solution of potash alum to the wound should stem the blood loss.

Egg-binding

This disorder can rapidly prove fatal and results from an egg becoming lodged in part of the reproductive tract. It is thus only seen in breeding hens, which appear fluffed-up and generally unsteady on their feet. A shortage of calcium, cold surroundings and immaturity of the bird concerned are all possible factors. The offending egg may only have a soft, rubbery shell which complicates the position, since it must not break within the bird's body as peritonitis is then likely to develop.

Raising the temperature alone, to about 30°C (85°F), may cause the egg to be passed within an hour or two. Alternatively, if there is no improvement, it must be removed by other means such as direct manipulation, surgery or an injection of calcium borogluconate, depending on the veterinarian's advice. Affected birds must not be allowed to breed for a year or so and the cause of the condition should be rectified where possible.

Digestive Problems

Candidiasis is caused by a yeast-like organism; affected birds are reluctant to swallow and appear to play with their food. Areas of white growth are likely to be evident in the mouth on close examination. This is a disease which rarely affects established stock but can be fatal if the growth spreads down into the crop and lower parts of the digestive tract. Eclectus and *Tanygnathus* parrots are at most risk, when their diet has been low in Vitamin A. Treatment consists of providing adequate supplementation of this vitamin in the first instance, often coupled with the use of a specific antibiotic for problems of mycotic (fungal) origin. Vitamin A is stored in the liver and the level of supplementation should be dramatically reduced once the condition is cured, since excessive levels can prove toxic. Regular daily feeding of greenstuff and similar items should ensure that the deficiency does not recur.

Digestive tract infections involving the intestines are usually described simply as 'enteritis'. It is difficult to determine the precise cause without laboratory tests and veterinary advice should be sought. It must not be forgotten that parrots, like most other creatures, can be afflicted with salmonellosis on occasions and this disease could be transmitted to humans, so that care needs to be taken when dealing with a parrot suffering from a severe digestive disturbance. Fluid must always be readily available because parrots with diarrhea, irrespective of the cause, will rapidly dehydrate and this by itself can prove fatal.

Feather Plucking

This vice is particularly common in parrots kept as pets and the reasons for such behavior are often difficult to establish and harder to remedy successfully. An inadequate diet, feather parasites, boredom, a desire to breed and other forms of stress can all be implicated. Treatment depends on isolating the underlying cause rapidly, before plucking becomes a habit. In severe cases with a pet bird, the only option will be to make contact with a sympathetic and knowledgeable breeder who may be able to assist in housing it out of doors with a mate.

Parasites

Red mite *Dermanyssus gallinae* is a relatively common parasite, living in the bird's immediate environment such as a nest-box. This parasite feeds on blood and can cause anemia, particularly in chicks, as well as a general loss of condition. All mites, as well as lice, are easily destroyed by means of a safe avian aerosol spray available from your local pet shop. Nest-boxes should be washed after the breeding season with a similar preparation as an additional precaution.

Intestinal worms can afflict parrots, especially those kept in aviaries with grass floors, which favor the survival of these worm eggs. Signs of infection are relatively non-specific, resulting overall in a lack of vigor. Examination of a fecal

The Thick-billed parrot from Mexico is the
only parrot to range into the USA.

ample under a microscope provides the best means of diagnosing the presence of
these parasites, with their eggs having a characteristic morphology. A veterinarian
can arrange for this to be carried out and provide appropriate medication. The
aviary itself will also need to be thoroughly cleaned using a blow-torch over the
surface, if necessary, to kill off any surviving eggs.

Respiratory Problems

As with enteritis, it is much easier to recognize the symptoms of breathing
disorders, rather than diagnosing their cause. This is a matter for a veterinarian.
Labored breathing is characterized by irregular, exaggerated tail movements and
wheezing may be audible. Bacteria and viruses may be implicated and fungi,
notably *Aspergillus*, can also be responsible. Recent research suggests that treatment of fungal disease using the human drug micronazole may at last be practical
in parrots and other birds.

In cases where the nostrils are blocked, this is indicative of sinusitis. Under these
circumstances, it is not unusual for one or both eyes to be involved as well. Eye
infections on their own usually respond readily with the use of an antibiotic
ophthalmic ointment or drops, which must be applied several times daily.

Bibliography

Alderton, D.   1982 *Parrots, Lories and Cockatoos,* Saiga Publishin
                             Hindhead, England

                             1984 *Howell Beginner's Guide to Cockatoos,* How
                             Book House, New York, New York, USA

                             1984 *Howell Beginner's Guide to Loverbirds,* How
                             Book House, New York, New York, USA

Bates, H.J. &   1969 *Parrots and related birds.* T.F.H. Pub. Neptu
Busenbark, R.   New Jersey, USA

Forshaw, J.M.   1973 *Parrots of the World, Landsdowne* Press. Melbour
                             Australia

Freud, A.   1980 *All About the Parrots,* Howell Book House, N
                             York, New York, USA

Gallerstein, G.A., DVM   1984 *Bird Owner's Home Health and Care Handboo
                             Howell Book House, New York, New York, USA

Harman, I.   1962 *Birdkeeping in Australia,* (Rev. Ed. 1978), Angus
                             Robertson, Sydney, Australia

Lendon, A.H.   1973 *Australian Parrots In Field and Aviary,* Angus a
                             Robertson, Sydney, Australia

Low, R.   1972 *The Parrots of South America,* John Giffor
                             London, England

                             1980 *Parrots–Their Care and Breeding,* Blandford Pre
                             Poole, England

                             1977 *Lories and Lorikeets,* Paul Elek, London, Engla

Rogers, C.   1984 *Howell Beginner's Guide to Cockatiels,* How
                             Book House, New York, New York, USA

Rutgers, A.   1972 *Encyclopaedia of Aviculture, Vol. 2,* Blandfo
                             Press, Pool, England

Vriends, Matthew M.   1983 *Popular Parrots,* Howell Book House, New Yor
                             New York, USA